INVITED TO SERVE

INVITED TO SERVE

HOW TO DISCERN GOD'S CALLING IN YOUR LIFE

22 People Share Their Stories

Dr. Gerald W. Bauer

Proclamation Strategies ✝ Solon, Ohio

INVITED TO SERVE
How To Discern God's Calling In Your Life

Copyright © 1998 by Gerald W. Bauer

ISBN   0-9659912-0-2
Library of Congress Catalog Card Number: 97-92606

Published by: Proclamation Strategies
32000 Arthur Road
Solon, Ohio 44139-4530

To the glory of God, reflected in the lives of the people
whose stories of calling are shared in this book

TABLE OF CONTENTS

PREFACE

Writing this book has been an overwhelming and humbling experience. The people I interviewed, whose stories of calling appear in these pages, have a passion for what they do. They all have a strong sense of God's call. They all give of themselves in many ways.

The author of a book is usually considered an expert in the field, the one who teaches others. My experience leads me to believe the people interviewed are the experts. I feel like they are teaching me. I hope you can learn from them, as I did, as you travel on your journey to discern God's calling in your life.

Many times while conducting the interviews I had the feeling I was standing on holy ground. These people shared how in special and specific ways God has touched their lives.

The people interviewed come from all walks of life with stories showing the variety of ways God leads people to their calling in life. A few had a clear sense of calling early in life. Most had to struggle and search.

I have used quotations extensively in the individual profiles. The intent is to reflect the people as much as possible, letting their own words and descriptive terms portray them.

In response to a number of inquiries and suggestions, I am including my own story of calling. I had not planned to do this since the book focuses on lay people and I am an ordained pastor. I hope my search for clarity of calling may be helpful to you.

The key to finding your calling, what God invites and equips you to do with your life, is to know yourself, to listen to your heart and follow it.

I am thankful to many people who helped make this book possible — to those who provided names of people to interview, ideas for categories of people to interview, and who offered encouragement and inspiration for me to write.

Special thanks goes to those who were so generous in interviews; to my wife, Sheri, for her ideas , her computer skills and for designing and typesetting the book; to Gloria Sladek for proofreading and editorial assistance; and to Bob Barstow for technical assistance and printing.

Gerald W. Bauer

Solon, Ohio

All Saints Day, November 1, 1997

INTRODUCTION

What does God call you to do with your life? How do you know when you find the thing that's right for you, what God has gifted you to do in life?

Do you ever find yourself feeling envious of a person who is doing what's right for them with a sense of joy and satisfaction? I sure do. How can I find that right niche for myself?

This book will help you answer these questions in two ways: First, it suggests ways to find the answer, and it provides resources that can help; second, it contains brief stories that highlight how Christians from all walks of life, in paid and in volunteer positions, have come to find their callings. The stories are designed to show the diverse ways these people came to discern their God given missions.

The search is a continuing process punctuated with joy and excitement as new discoveries are made and opportunities unfold. It's an open ended creative journey that brings freshness and vitality to life. For some there is a single destination. For others the destination reached today is but the jump-off point for the destinations of tomorrow and the tomorrow after that.

The process is a spiritual journey toward God in whose image we are created. This God sends us into the world gifted for a mission that we uniquely can do.

Seeking to find what you want to do with your life, your calling, requires answers to several questions. What are your gifts? What needs do you see that call for your gifts? How do you get from where you are now into a position, paid or volunteer, that addresses the needs that can be met with your gifts?

The questions are easy. Finding the answers is not. Honesty with yourself in dealing with the issues raised is crucial to satisfactory and satisfying results: knowing your gifts, where you want to use them, and how to get there.

Read through this book quickly to get an overview of what's here. Then read slowly taking time to stop and reflect. You will probably want to make notes of your reflections and insights as you read.

From the profiles of the people interviewed, narrow your focus to the ones that best relate to you. The profiles include people in an age range from teenager to the eighties; those who were clear about their calling early in life to those whose quest is ongoing; those who have struggled long and hard; those who have endured difficult times. A broad range of the ways people have come to discern their calling in life is represented. What can you learn from their experiences? What ideas emerge from their stories that help you find answers to your questions?

God bless your journey.

Called By God

In the beginning God created human beings, gave them freedom to make decisions, and placed them in the world to manage it according to God's intent. Work was good, creativity important, and individual responsibility a must. I believe this is true for life today.

Everyone has their own unique personality, abilities, and interests which together form their giftedness. I give the term "gift" this broad definition.

Identity as a gifted person begins in God. Being created in the image of God influences the process used to discover gifts and how and where they will be used. Who God is says something about who you are.

God's self introduction to Moses, variously translated as "I am who I am," or "I will be who I will be," portrays God as a free, self determined, and self defining being. If God is a free God, then you, created in God's image are a free person. You are free to make decisions about the discovery of your gifts and how you will use them.

God respects your freedom and creativity. After all, God created you that way. God does not dictate what you should do. Rather, God invites you into the joy of self discovery.

It's natural to want all the answers right away. Rarely do things come clear quickly for a person. Seek God's guidance and direction. Prayer, meditation, silence, and reflection are essential to hearing what God has to say and seeing what God has to show you. To search for your calling in life is to take a deeply spiritual journey. It is, above all else, a religious quest.

How To Discern Your Gifts And Call

Here's an exercise you can use to start your journey of self discovery. Take some paper and mark off four columns. From the left side of the page label the first column "experience," the second column "abilities used," the third "values," and the fourth "interests."

Next, divide your life into three to five year segments beginning with your earliest recollections. Vary the time spans to what makes the most sense for you.

First, in the "experience" column list the things you have done. They can be accomplishments, activities, hobbies, jobs, volunteer work, travel, and anything else you want to add.

Second, in the "abilities" column note the abilities you used in each of the things you did. Abilities include: analyze, compute, speak, write, persuade, sell, counsel, plan, organize, construct, work with hands, mechanical, etc. When you have finished your list review it and identify the abilities that occur most frequently. You should find a pattern. There will be certain abilities that you used more than others. These are a clue to your giftedness.

Still working in the "abilities" column narrow your list to the few abilities which, when you use them, motivate you to use them more. Intercristo, a Christian organization which works with people making career decisions, calls these abilities your "motivated abilities." These are crucial to your calling. They must be part of whatever you do in order for you to find satisfaction. They are gifts you have.

Third, in the values column identify your most important values. Values include such things as independence, security, creativity, honesty, learning, like or dislike of change, like or dislike of structured settings, freedom, risk taking, and safety.

You might just make a single list or you may identify the values that were important in each experience you listed. The end results should be the same. Your values must be incorporated into any satisfying work.

Fourth, in the interests column list your significant interests. What interested you in each experience you listed? What do you enjoy and what do you enjoy doing? You can also include types of places you like to be. This information will help define the setting or context in which you would find the greatest satisfaction.

While this approach depends on having considerable life experience from which to draw, another route to self discovery is possible. I believe the seeds of giftedness are present early on — from the beginning of life.

For young people who do not have a wealth of life experience to draw on, let me suggest another approach. Others may want to do this as well.

What have you day dreamed about doing with your life? Have you fantasized about the work, position, or ideal situation in life you would really like to see for yourself? Often, early ideas about what people want to do are put down by parents, teachers or others as impractical, too expensive, or with the comment, "you're just not good enough to do this."

Take your day dreams or fantasies and recall them. Imagine yourself doing what you really want. What activities are you performing? What skills, abilities, gifts are you using? What is it that interests you about your vision for yourself? What in your dreams motivates and excites you? Answering these questions will give you clues to your gifts and your calling.

A number of resources are available to help you identify your interests, abilities, values, and personality. How effective they are for you depends on how honest you are with yourself.

Let me use myself as an example of how not to do this. At one time business management models were suggested by a few people as holding great promise for the church. The concept of the pastor executive gained some popularity.

Think about the symbolism in the term executive. The thoughts of power, prestige, and a position with good pay sure sounded good to me. Besides, if things did not work out in the church, management skills could easily transfer to the corporate office.

I pursued management studies and positions that would put me in a management setting, such as senior pastor of a congregation. I also started working through career guidance books, beginning with Richard Bolles, *What Color is Your Parachute?* More self analysis, career counseling, and use of tests followed. All seemed to support management as a viable career focus, in or outside of the church.

As I incorporated management tools into my work as pastor, I became aware that things were not working the way they were supposed to work. Of course, it was not my fault.

Over time I came to realize that I was not doing what successful managers do. I knew the right answers but my giftedness did not equip me for implementing them. It took some time for me to admit that I did not have the gift of management.

While difficult, this admission did two things. It freed me from moving towards positions that would be frustrating and end in failure. Second, it freed me to be open and honest with myself as I pursued my real gifts.

The point in sharing this is to show that the answers you want from self assessment tools are the answers you will get. It's easy to answer the questions in ways that support your desired outcome.

The only right answers point you to become the person God uniquely created you to be. The only right type of work, paid or volunteer, is the work, position, or career in which you can use your giftedness to its fullest. This means being honest with yourself.

Knowing your gifts keeps you from going after interesting opportunities which are dead end streets. They may be right for others, but they are not right for you because you do not have the gifts for them.

I took side tracks many times. They were interesting, but frustrating because they were not right for me. Various opportunities will come along. They may be exciting. They may promise riches, prestige, and a bright future to all who follow them. But unless it's right for you, it will not satisfy and it will not deliver what it seems to promise.

Therefore, let go of things that are not really you, that do not utilize your motivated abilities. Instead of coming up empty, you will move closer to your real giftedness.

Another help in discovering giftedness is finding and responding to needs and opportunities that call for your gifts. Look around you. What needs do you see? Do any of them generate a sense of urgency in you? Do you find yourself saying, "I can do something about that?"

Keeping a journal also provides a good way to get in touch with yourself, your giftedness, your sense of calling, and to experience God's guiding. Writing forces you to clarify your thinking. The journal gives you opportunity to review days, weeks, and months of thoughts and ideas. You see what stays the same, what strengthens, and what gets discarded. I find this helpful, especially when considering direction for my life.

Journal keeping need not be difficult. Do it your own way. Whether you write a couple of sentences or a couple of pages is up to you. Write daily, weekly, or sporadically. Only what works best for you matters.

In your journal record your thoughts, ideas, questions, concerns, insights, and reflections. Write for yourself. For a concise guide to journal writing see Ronald Klug's book, *How to Keep a Spiritual Journal.*

Another clue to giftedness can come from other people, especially people of faith. They may see what you do not see. Insights from these people can confirm gifts. They can also question if you have a certain gift.

When giftedness is discovered all approaches lead to it. It feels right, satisfying, and comfortable. There will be a sense of "this is what I need to be doing."

The doing may not be easy. Once you discover what you are called to do, you need to find ways to do it. The way may be a paid or volunteer position. You may need a regular job to support your calling. If the perfect situation is not available, make sure any position you take moves you closer to it. An alternative is to create your own business or position.

Focusing Your Call

The discovery of giftedness continues through life. Because you are a growing and subsequently changing person, the gifts discernment process means you are open to see new signs of giftedness. If you have been honest with yourself, these new signs will expand upon and be consistent with what is already in place. You may feel called to use your gifts in a new setting. Or, you may see how your gifts can relate in different ways. Changes in life will be seen as opportunity to experience new joy in who you are and how you are gifted.

Developing a personal calling statement may help bring gifts and their applications together. Do not try to create a literary masterpiece. A list or short phrases will do. Do this for yourself and no one else. Use the statement to focus the direction of your life. Use the following five questions as a guide.

1. Who are you? You may use your values to identify who you are. As an alternative, use of instruments like the Myers Briggs Type Indicator can help. Gary Harbaugh leads readers through a simplified version in his book, *God's Gifted People*. I used this and found it accurate. The illustrations for each personality type show what the person may be doing in life.

2. What are your gifts? Use the insights about your motivated abilities. How do they mesh with your personality?

3. In what ways can you use your giftedness? List all situations that could make use of your gifts. Which ones interest you the most? Do any make you feel "this is what I ought to be doing?" Your sense of calling may begin to emerge.

4. Who will you serve with your giftedness? Get more specific about the use of your gifts. Identify the people in your preferred situations that could benefit from your gifts.

5. In what settings? What type of setting do you prefer? Paid or volunteer? Working for an organization or for yourself? Church related or secular? Answers to these and other setting questions help clarify how your gifts can be used.

Knowing you giftedness gives direction in seeking career or service, whether paid or volunteer. You express and use your gifts through what you do. Work becomes more than just a job. Volunteer positions are more than just something to keep busy, or because "they need somebody over here."

Your giftedness gives meaning and purpose to your life. It forms your sense of calling. Your giftedness is your call from God. It is your invitation to serve God.

Finding your calling in life is an exciting process. It also contains a trap. You may be tempted to keep discovering. The discovery process can become an excuse not to act. The additional insights you want may not appear. The temptation is to delay until you have perfect information. Your life can come to a standstill. Nothing happens.

There comes a time to make a decision, commit to it, and act on it. The picture you want may not be perfectly clear. What you see may not result in an exclamation, "this is it." To wait for a crystal clear picture may prevent you from acting at all.

At some point decisions must be made about what fits and what does not fit. The case may be that the gifts are clear but the setting is not clear.

It may help to form a vision of using your gifts in your ideal setting. Put it into words. Your vision becomes a goal.

What do you need to do to reach it? What steps do you need to take to get there? What changes do you have to make? What risks do you have to take?

Once convinced that you have made the right choice, commit yourself and your resources to it. It's your life. It's your future. It's your dream. It's your identity. It's your calling. Make a pledge to yourself that your are going to do this.

Next, take action. Do it now, not later, because later usually means nothing happens. It helps to set deadlines. As you act, let people know where you are headed and what you want to do. As you do this other parts of the picture will fall into place.

If all this sounds risky, it is. But it's a bigger risk to do nothing, to accept what life hands you. The saddest thing to see is someone toward the end of life saying, "I wish I had done this," or "if I had done that, I might have been." That person feels cheated out of a satisfying life.

True, you will run across naysayers, people who would steal your dream, your identity, and your calling. Ignore them. They are usually people who have no sense of their own identity and calling. Those who do have a vision for their own lives will be glad to help you achieve yours.

Move forward in faith. Live toward the vision of the future God gives you. Use your giftedness to help create it. Keep the momentum going.

Evaluate the course of your life on a continuing basis. Be aware of signs or input that reinforce your direction, or that could mean it's time to look at some changes.

Giftedness will remain fairly constant. You may find new needs that make use of your gifts. A change in setting may be appropriate. Or, a different combination of your gifts may be needed.

Be flexible and open to new opportunities and discoveries. Stay alert to new ventures that God uses to call you to be more the person God created you to be.

Diana I. Barton, R.N.
Parish Nurse

Diana Barton describes her calling to nursing with a feeling of commitment, purpose and enthusiasm for her work. She sees nursing as more than a job, and more as an art than a science. As a teenager Barton lived near a hospital. She volunteered as a candy striper and gradually came to sense that nursing was her calling.

Barton's instructors in nursing school were caring people. They helped her understand that she needed to know the sciences, but that caring for patients was important. "Caring for people was the highlight of my training," said Barton. "I learned most by doing."

Faith finds expression in various situations and work settings for Barton. Her prayer life was important at an early age and has continued to grow stronger. Church was always important for her.

Barton has worked in an emergency service, for a surgeon, and in industrial medicine. When her children were small she stayed home with them, yet she served the neighborhood. The neighbors knew she was a nurse and often called her with questions.

While working at a nursing facility, Barton's pastor asked if she had ever heard of parish nursing and invited her to go to a conference. When she moved to the Cleveland area seven years ago her new pastor asked if she had ever considered parish nursing. As a result Barton began to do parish nursing. The parish nurse is Christian oriented nursing, and includes a large spiritual component.

"My life is one of service," says Barton. "That service has been a joy whether family or professionally oriented.

Spiritual orientation has always been an important part of my life, especially in making decisions. I can look over my life and see how the Lord was working."

Barton has always kept a prayer journal. She has been able to look back and see different ways her prayers have been answered. She also reflects that there have been some prayers with no apparent answers. Barton's journal allows her to follow her journey and to see growth in her life.

"I really feel like the Lord is using me for good," states Barton. "As I look back in my life I feel there has been a reason for everything. My medical background, my family, and knowing the Lord is with me have helped during trying times."

"I feel so blessed to be able to do this health ministry," says Barton. "Parish nursing is growing. It can be church, hospital, or community based." Being a parish nurse means meeting all the requirements for hospital nursing, having state certificates, and having malpractice insurance.

As a parish nurse, "I try to help people pull on their faith to deal with a medical or psychological problem," says Barton. "I pray with people. I have seen a lot of things over time that reinforced my faith."

Some of the more frequent things Barton does as a parish nurse include: health education through the congregation's educational system; teaching subjects on fitness, healthy hearts, self esteem, skin care and cancer; blood pressure screening; forums on living wills, organ donation, and medical durable power of attorney in conjunction with experts in these fields; hospital and nursing home visits; going to the doctor with elderly people and helping them to understand what was said; taking part in a service of healing with the pastor; and individual consultations.

Among her gifts, Barton says that other people have recognized in her a gift for listening without being judgmental. Other gifts she was able to name, using a gifts discovery questionnaire, include showing mercy and compassion, intercession, healing, and wisdom — all gifts she uses as a parish nurse.

Stephen Battles, D.O.
Physician

Dr. Stephen Battles sees his calling in two ways. He considers his work as a physician his specific calling, serving God by attending to the physical needs of his patients. He also sees his calling encompassing all of his life, living as a Christian, reflecting Christian values in all that he does. "You can't separate medical practice and issues from the Christian faith," says Battles. "Life's problems and medical practice come together."

Among his gifts, Battles names patience, both with people and with his own shortcomings. Patience helps him stick to what he does. It helped him get through medical school. Another gift is intelligence, especially important in medical education. A third gift is the will to succeed. This gift helps to keep him on track. Battles says he always enjoyed the sciences, even as a child. He was very clear about what he did and did not like in school. He geared his high school classes around science.

Battles interest in medicine came early in his life. His family doctor served as a role model. He told the doctor of his interest in medicine and was encouraged to pursue it. Following medical school, his first year residency was spent working in his family doctor's practice.

During high school, Battles volunteered to work in the emergency room of the local hospital. He enjoyed being at the hospital. The surgeons asked him if he wanted to scrub and help with surgery. This experience affirmed his interest in medicine.

"I am very satisfied with what I'm doing," says Battles. "I started early and stayed on track. I was very confident this is what I wanted to do." Battles says there were a couple of obstacles to overcome in getting to college, but he was so focused he didn't let it get him off track.

"I am affirmed in my calling to be a physician by the joy I feel in what I do," declares Battles. "There comes an occasional bad day, or some office politics, but it's no big deal." Delivering babies, helping to bring new life into the world, is a special joy for Battles. Seeing people who are sick or injured get better also brings satisfaction. Battles likes the fact that he sees immediate results from his work.

Church was always a focal point in Battles' life. It gave him spiritual strength to pursue his interest in a medical career. It remains important in his life today.

Battles' mother, a strong willed, hard worker, often working at several jobs, provides a role model for his own determination to succeed. She was an influence in his life that helped him to stay focused on his career goal.

Battles is a person for whom Christian faith expresses itself in all dimensions of life. His faith influences who he is, what he does, and how he practices medicine. He cannot separate faith and life. Battles' faith reaches into every aspect of his life — at home, at church, in the community, in his medical practice.

Josiah H. Blackmore, II
University President

When he was six years old, Josiah Blackmore's father told him that he wanted him to be a lawyer. "And I wanted to be a lawyer," says Blackmore, with enthusiasm in his voice. "My father was very structured in terms of his expectations for me. He was self read, self educated, loved to talk philosophy, enjoyed intellectual discussions, a brilliant person. But he was not religious in the traditional sense."

Early in his high school years Blackmore became active in a congregation. He began thinking about ministry as a career, although law remained his major focus. His father suggested he attend high school at Admiral Farragut Academy in preparation for the U.S. Naval Academy at Annapolis, then go to law school.

Blackmore's heroes during these formative years were Peter Marshall, chaplain of the United States Senate and popular preacher, and Daniel Poling whose son was one of the four chaplains immortalized after giving up their life jackets so others could live when the troop ship Dorchester was sunk by a Nazi torpedo. The idea of ministry returned and strengthened.

While home for a vacation Blackmore voiced his interest in the ministry. He decided to spend his senior year at Kent State University High School in Kent, Ohio, still thinking of ministry and law.

At Miami University, Blackmore majored in government. The writings of Paul Tillich and Reinhold Niebuhr, prominent theologians, helped him relate faith, intellect and reason. Fulfillment of part of his original plan came with service in the U.S. Navy and graduation from The Ohio State University

College of Law. On becoming a member of the bar, Blackmore's practice focused on helping poor people through legal services. He realized this too was a form of ministry.

Blackmore saw serving people as a key to his calling. This serving took the form of teaching, transferring his commitment to care and concern for his students. Blackmore was offered an adjunct faculty position at the Capital University Law School. He found teaching a real joy, the teaching of law very fulfilling. He became professor of law and then dean of the law school.

"My faith was rooted through my experiences," said Blackmore, "but it was Capital University that began to help me reform my faith into a mature faith. People at Capital University were formative for me." The sermons of his own pastor also nurtured his faith.

The idea of going into the ministry still persisted for Blackmore. Even as dean of the law school, he contemplated going to seminary when his service there was completed. Instead, Capital University called him to be president.

Blackmore continued to nurture his faith through his associations with Capital's campus pastor, religion faculty, and the president and faculty at Trinity Lutheran Seminary, located adjacent to Capital University. "This setting is my seminary and my ministry," says Blackmore. "This fits with who I am."

Students often come to campus with their lives broken, lacking direction, and needing help. Blackmore's office door is open to them. This is ministry. "Capital reaches out to students," says Blackmore. "It doesn't push them out." He expresses a deeply caring compassion for the well being of students.

Concern for students includes caring for their academic development. A commitment to compassion is matched by a commitment to intellectual pursuits. For example, Blackmore reflected, "I would like to write something about the saint-hood of unbelievers, because I have seen profound articles of faith disguised in the writings of those who supposedly do not believe. Are they religious but call it by a different name?" For instance, he refers to the English author Thomas Hardy, an agnostic buried in Westminster Abbey. In Hardy's *Far From the Madding Crowd*, Blackmore sees a joining of the temporal and the eternal in farmer Oakes who tells time by the stars and a pocket watch lacking an hour hand. "He is so theological," says Blackmore. "I think God speaks through this agnostic."

Another influential insight came to Blackmore at a Lutheran Educational Conference in North America. A campus pastor and religion professor at Wartburg College, Waverly, Iowa, said in a lecture, "what I like to talk with students about is the infallibility of the Bible, not as history but as metaphor. Christ taught using metaphors." Blackmore is fond of the biblical story of the prophet Jonah, a righteous person who fled from God's call. The whale represents the consequence of fleeing. Jonah comes out of the belly of the whale when in faith he calls to God for help. Blackmore sees a lot of people who live like the biblical prophet Jonah. "They are righteous, good people," says Blackmore, "but they busy themselves with doing everything except what they are called to do. This gives rise to an anguish cured only by returning to God, in faithfulness to God's call, seeking God's help."

"The cross," says Blackmore, "invites people to say, 'help me.' The cross also expresses that it's permissible to be imperfect." One of his favorite Scripture passages is, "Lord I believe, help my unbelief."

Bonnie Boots
Writer, Artist

My wife, Sheri, "met" Bonnie Boots in a forum for doll makers on the Internet. After several months, I would have defined her gifts as a sense of humor and a generous sharing spirit. I cannot add anything to her response to a request for an interview, so this is what Bonnie Boots said:

When I was a child, adults exclaimed over my "natural talent" for drawing and writing. I exploited these talents (I found I could get out of gym class to decorate the school's display case, for instance) but I didn't take my abilities seriously. They came so easily to me, seemingly without effort, that I didn't feel any sense of "ownership" about them. They weren't something I'd earned, with sweat and effort, just something that was born with me, like my brown hair. They scared me a little, too. I was both proud and appalled to be so different from everyone else.

As I grew older, I found my abilities were worth something in the market place, and I sold them where I could. I used them the way a farmer might use a mule he found wild in his fields. I roped them and trained them to perform in a useful way. It was all the same to me if I wrote menus or poetry, and I was equally amazed that anyone would pay me for either. I felt guilty, accepting money for something I hadn't really "earned," as my friends earned money for real work, like baby-sitting or cashiering. Lacking respect for my gifts, I squandered them, and for many years didn't use them at all.

When I was thirty eight years old, I was seriously injured in an auto accident. I left home one beautiful fall day, when the air was as crisp and ripe as a Vermont apple, and headed for the beach. I was a business owner, happily married, successful, intelligent, secure. When I returned home, I was broken in body and spirit. Injuries to my brain and spine left me bedridden for the next two years, with chronic pain that has lessened, but never departed. During those two crippled years, nearly everything I thought defined me drifted away. I lost my business, my financial assets, my social status, my friends, my physical attractiveness, my sense of self-worth. Those things I thought gave value and meaning to my life were stripped away, like leaves off a branch, until all that was left was the naked, shivering twig.

It was then, with everything else cleared away, that I saw my life for what it was...the wasteland where I had allowed my gifts to wither. I did clearly see them then, my inborn talents, as gifts that had been bestowed on me, and the regret I felt for wasting them was vast and bitter. I wallowed in depression , disgust and regret for a long, long time; wallowed there until I was exhausted. It was then, from the depths of despair, that I made a vow to myself to find whatever remnants of those gifts might still remain, and nourish them. It was that vow, and that determination, that pulled me out of bed, and set me on the path that brought me to the work I do today.

I started small. On weekends, when I felt able, my husband took me to a flea market where I drew caricatures for a dollar. The first time a man sat down before my easel my hand shook so badly I couldn't control my pen. Only my determination kept me from running away. Within two months my caricatures were attracting such attention I was offered a job at a major theme park. I couldn't accept, because of my health challenges, but the offer gave me confidence to move ahead. I designed and sold a cartoon strip to a magazine. A few months later I wrote several articles. Bit by bit, I nurtured my talents, giving them time and room to grow in whatever way they could. Because I'd been unable to work for so long, I now cherished every opportunity to work. I gave myself permission to have bad days, and felt vastly grateful for good ones.

Today, nine years after that accident, I have a life I once barely dreamed of. My articles and art work have been published in many national magazines and several books. My days are overcrowded with my work as a newspaper editor and columnist, as well as artist, and I have opportunities to speak and teach all around the world. These days, laying in bed is not a curse, but a rare luxury.

My life is not what anyone but me would think of as "normal." Because time spent housekeeping is time robbed from my studio, anyone dropping in is in danger of being lost amidst an avalanche of books, manuscripts, paints, clays and fabrics. Only my work writing restaurant reviews allows my husband and I to have proper meals on a regular basis. I make no excuses. I have tremendous respect for the creative gifts the Maker has given me and apologize to no one for living differently in order to explore them. I AM different. I am one of an infinitely small group of human beings blessed with the ability to take up a scrap of cloth, a daub of paint, a bit of wood, a wad of clay, a pen, and conjure from them something that existed only in thought until their hands gave it form. Creativity is a sacred act that requires chaos, laughter, courage and isolation. Those who choose service in its temple must sacrifice at its altar, sacrifice the easy path of the status quo, the comfort and security of the common life. Only those who make the sacrifices, who do service in their own messy temples, who live independent of the good opinion of others, who suffer the pains of isolation and insecurity in order to create, only they ever stand at the end of the journey, illuminated in the presence of the ultimate Maker of Things and understand how blessed they have been to share in the act of Creation.

George W. Cochran, Jr.
Attorney

George Cochran sees his calling as a Christian lawyer. He envisions expanding his law practice through the development of a Church Law Center. He would provide various levels of legal services , including conflict resolution, to member congregations of the Center, and eventually function as a church management consultant.

Following graduation from college and law school, Cochran began a successful banking career and became more actively involved in the church he attended. Eventually, he sensed a call to attend seminary, a key event in discerning his calling. He felt God was calling him and his family to service in Russia following graduation. He had no intention of practicing law.

At seminary he focused his study in church administration. By graduation time he sensed that God was closing the door to service in Russia. This was a difficult time. He had felt strongly that mission work in Russia was his calling.

He began to think of returning to his native Streetsboro, Ohio. He came to realize that God was calling him to open a law practice. He did not understand why, but he began to see a wonderful application of his gifts of leadership and administration, affirmed during his term as president of the Chamber of Commerce.

With his law practice firmly established, Cochran is beginning work on the Church Law Center. His calling becomes more specific as he pursues what he discerns God wants him to do.

Cochran talks about the Christian's calling. The primary general call is "to be a faithful disciple of the Lord Jesus Christ as he gives me opportunity moment to moment," says Cochran.

"God invites us to have part in his work." He sees his "number one ministry to be a godly husband and father."

After the door to Russia closed, his sense of call became very general, leading him to be "receptive to whatever God calls me to do." Then the calling started to get specific again. It became like a camera lens bringing the subject into focus.

Go back to Streetsboro. Open a law practice. Begin working on the Church Law Center. The specific call for Cochran comes within the context of the general call of God. "As long as you try to focus on a specific call and gifts God can't totally use you because you skip the general call. Let go of specifics and be open," declares Cochran. "Surrender to God and God will give you the specific call. When you stop needing to be specifically used, now I (God) can specifically use you."

Cochran sees the gifts of the Holy Spirit in a broader sense than just those gifts listed in the New Testament. "If you define gifts too narrowly," says Cochran, "you miss opportunities."

The first clue Cochran had for his gifts and calling came as he began to question decisions made by the leadership of his congregation. The gifts were affirmed during his time at seminary, especially by the dean who had the same gifts. She encouraged him to pursue his gifts. This excited him and motivated him to use his gifts as he followed God's calling. Another important influence in Cochran's life came from a fellow church administration student. The student, from Kenya, helped him to see the importance of being, to see who he is as a person. He describes himself as "a leader in administration, to help visionary leaders turn their visions into reality."

William E. Diehl
Management Consultant

William Diehl, founder and president of Riverbend Resource Center, provides management consulting services for both businesses and nonprofit organizations. He began his consulting practice after leaving a position as a national sales manager for Bethlehem Steel Corporation.

Diehl's twenty-two years of continuous high level institutional church experience includes service on the church councils of the Lutheran Church in America and its successor body, the Evangelical Lutheran Church in America. He played an instrumental role in the formation of the ELCA (January 1, 1987), serving on the Commission of Seventy that did the organizing work.

His calling focuses on connecting Sunday faith with the weekday world. He helps people relate their experience of Sunday worship with their experience of weekday work. He finds that his experience in the world of work gives him credibility in the church. His experience in the church gives him credibility in the business and nonprofit sectors.

Diehl points to several ways he carries out his calling. In his congregation Diehl organized the Center for Faith and Life which does the programming for Sunday morning adult forums. Programs focus on issues people encounter during the week. The issues are addressed in the context of a biblical and theological forum.

Programs involve a series of month long issue groups. Two series run concurrently. Usually on the first Sunday a professional theologian brings a biblical and theological orientation to the issue. On the following Sundays other experts from such fields as health care, business, the judicial system, education and others bring their perspectives to the issue. For example, on the issues of doctor assisted suicide and the rationing of health care, physicians addressed the group. About 100 people attend.

Another way Diehl implements his calling is through the Monday Connection. This breakfast discussion group meets at a restaurant from 7 to 8 a.m. the first Monday of the month. One person volunteers to share a real life case study of an issue current for them. The group raises questions and shares insights in order to help the presenter see options in resolving the issue. No one is ever told what to do. The pastor attends as both participant and resident theologian to offer biblical connections. Attendance averages thirty persons.

Diehl also promotes a course called Connections, published by the Evangelical Lutheran Church in America. It consists of twenty weekly meetings and two retreat weekends. The first part of the course focuses on what faith says about daily life. Resources include the creeds of the church and Luther's Small Catechism. The second part has participants visit the work place of group members who explain what they do. They describe how faith connects with their work. The others comment on how they can see God's work being done. The ideal group size is twelve to fifteen.

Diehl also expresses his calling through involvement in such community groups as the Community Action Committee of Lehigh Valley, the Lehigh County Housing Authority and the Interfaith Coalition on Poverty. Through them he uses his organizational gift to help address poverty issues and to monitor the new welfare policy to see what other hurts it might create.

Diehl sees his greatest gift as his ability to organize. He likes to start things and follow through with them. Positive feedback from his work and his involvement in community groups reinforce his sense of giftedness.

Writing as another gift finds expression in the seven books Diehl has written. He discovered this gift when a friend suggested he put the thoughts he was expressing about faith and life into a book. *Christianity and Daily Life*, published in 1976, went into seven printings and was a Fortress Press best seller.

Diehl describes the discernment of his calling and gifts as a gradual process. The wide acceptance of his first book was an important clue. He heard people saying, "you've written what we've been thinking."

Diehl encountered his first major occupational decision point on his way up the corporate ladder at Bethlehem Steel. He had to decide if he was a captive of the corporation and accept moving anywhere the company said he should move. Offered a major promotion involving a move, which would be hard on his family, he said, "no." At that time such a response was unthinkable.

Two things resulted from his decision. First, he felt very liberated, knowing he could place family interests ahead of career. Second, he did eventually receive a promotion without having to relocate.

Another major decision came as Diehl realized he did not want to work for one company all his life. He desired to do consulting work with both small businesses and nonprofit organizations. This meant leaving Bethlehem Steel and founding Riverbend Resource Center.

Two people, through their books, had an impact on Diehl's life. He heard from the Bible and the pulpit such things as unlimited forgiveness, and that the first shall be last and the last first. He struggled as to what the Bible might mean for his life as a salesman. He found no help from the church, an extremely frustrating circumstance. Help came from Elton Trueblood whose books came along just as Diehl needed them.

Another influential person was Mark Gibbs, author of *God's Frozen People*. This, Diehl says, "was the 'aha' book." Gibbs portrayed God's people as frozen by the institution of the church. Gibbs connected with Diehl's experience. Gibbs sequel book, *God's Lively People*, gave hope for the future.

Insights from Trueblood and Gibbs set Diehl on his way, using his gifts of organizing and writing, to implement his calling of helping people connect Sunday faith and daily life. His books on faith and life are widely read. He is a popular speaker throughout the church, an affirmation of his calling.

Bradley S. Doll
Theater President

"I depend on God's daily provision and direction in my life," says an energetic Bradley Doll. "I follow the Scriptural admonition to trust in the Lord, the Lord who promises to direct my paths and order my steps."

Doll's calling to write, produce and direct, to the glory of God, finds expression in The Doll House Theater. Short term, he envisions a community theater, arts, music, and dance. Longer term, he will create video productions and a video data base club, direct marketing videos to families. Phase three of his plan focuses on writing and producing films for families on the big screen.

Doll also created Doll House Enterprises as a for profit diversified agency. His dream includes an entertainment agency, talent agency, advertising agency, promotions, direct mail, public relations, media services, graphic design and production, writing, producing, directing, sales meetings, wedding receptions, meetings, banquets, lodging, a gift shop and art gallery.

Doll identifies a number of gifts, including the gift of dreams and visions, saying "God has given me the ability to see things that don't exist." Another gift includes writing. He is a published poet, has produced advertising in the print media, and wants to write scripts. Additional gifts include analytical and strategic thinking, public speaking, interpersonal skills, empathy toward people and an obsession for giving. He loves to help people.

Doll has come to focus his calling in his areas of interest. "There is power in serving God through my interests," states Doll. "I have been lead from marketing to advertising to writing to art directing to theater."

For Doll, "there are too many walking dead people. They go to work, but they don't like it. Joy comes from serving God in your area of interest," says Doll. "You have much more power and energy."

Doll said he "was saved in 1989." His step mother, a strong Christian, was killed in an accident by a drunk driver while in the process of leaving his alcoholic father. "At her funeral I realized the poverty of what I had as life's purpose. Even my Harvard education and prestigious career did not prepare me to face death. I knew the Lord was real. In desperation I called out to Christ to save me, and I gave my life to Christ."

When Procter & Gamble let him go, Doll decided to go to Bible college. God closed the doors. Neither could he get into any of dozens of Christian ministries for which he applied. Broken, he didn't know what to do.

Doll took a job with Iams Pet Food Company. "I thought this was a dirty job compared to serving God," pointed out Doll. "I heard a James Dobson program focusing on how God used animals to comfort people." That changed his perception of his job.

Doll tried other ministries again. Nothing worked. He took a prestigious job at another large firm. He still was not satisfied that he was doing what he needed to do to serve God.

"I bought a book about finding God's will," said Doll. "I read the Bible, prayed, and sought counsel from mature Christian people. I came to see that God creates circumstances in life to direct people. At times, God may dry up provisions as a sign that it's time to move on to something else. The final advice from the book was to follow your heart's desire."

"If you seek to please God, he will stir up your desires and empower you to do them," declares Doll. "I had the desire to write, direct and produce movies." He questioned whether this was of the Lord. The church he attended believed going to movies was a sin. A week long Christian film festival in town cleared his mind. He saw "that many people turned to the Lord after viewing these Christian films."

After he finished reading the book about knowing God's will, Doll prayed "that, if his desire was God's will, that God would open the door." He began praying in October. In November the prayer was answered by a job offer from Grey Advertising in Los Angeles. He had prayed for more money. The salary was an increase of 50 percent. He also received a double promotion, to vice president. He began to do what he desired to do, working for the fifth largest advertising firm in the world.

Another move took Doll to the third largest agency, but his wife wanted to go back to Ohio. Her father had recently accepted a call to pastor a church in Norwalk, Ohio, and said there was a theater where Doll could do his writing, producing and directing. The day before the Dolls left for a two week vacation in Ohio, Doll was informed that his job was being terminated. He interprets this as God showing the way. He found a new job, created just for him, with a significant salary increase, at an agency in Cleveland.

The final affirmation, that Doll's desires to use his gifts to serve God were right, came when he met with the executive director of the Norwalk theater. They hit it off. The theater had been doing wholesome family programming. Doll formed his two corporations, The Doll House Theater as a nonprofit, and Doll House Enterprises as a for profit venture.

With some doubts remaining, Doll prayed "for a final, miraculous kind of answer that would show him for certain he was on the right track." The Cleveland agency let him go. The job created just for him was gone. The company was downsizing, he was told. But, he was the only one downsized. "This was not the answer I anticipated," says Doll, "but it was God's way of showing me clearly that I should pursue my heart's desire."

Robert Everhart
Volunteer Service

Robert Everhart speaks confidently about his calling to service. "Reading about the gifts of the Spirit in the Bible, I've come to believe that service is my calling, and it can show up in a lot of different ways," says Everhart. "I see most of the things I do as some form of service."

"Jesus said he came to serve, not to be served, and the same applies to us," states Everhart. "Christ's life is a role model showing how he helped people in all kinds of ways. Service means helping people who need God's help through you."

One service Everhart renders, along with his wife Margie, is a music ministry to residents at a nursing home. He leads a monthly sing-a-long. It started when he went with a group of people from church to sing for the residents. "I can sing and I have a strong voice so I became song leader," says Everhart. "We sing favorite requests. When there are none, which happens often, we indirectly spread the gospel by suggesting religious songs. We also use light-hearten humor and ham it up. We try to get people to enjoy the hour we are there."

"I found that if you treat people in the nursing home like anyone else, they respond," declares Everhart. "Treat the people as though they were normal even if they have disabilities. They respond. They like you."

Everhart also visits residents at another nursing home in the area, and home bound people from church. He provides care for these elderly people, letting them know somebody is interested. "A lot of my service is directed to senior citizens,," says Everhart. "It didn't start out that way, but I went where the need was and it was with the elderly."

Everhart serves his church by singing in the choir, working on the fellowship and vision committees, and helping to host a community Thanksgiving dinner to which nursing home residents are invited. He also helps bring those same residents to a Palm Sunday worship service at his church, followed by a luncheon.

As for giftedness, the gift of singing goes along with Everhart's gift of serving. He recalls singing since his junior high school days both in school and in church. He can read music, but he has no professional training.

Everhart also names his sense of humor as a gift. "I can tell people things and get away with it when nobody else could," says Everhart. "It's an ice breaker. I can get close to people quickly, and it helps me to meet new people in church. It makes it easier to remember names, and is a way to keep a conversation flowing."

"Spreading the gospel and helping people seems natural to me," notes Everhart. "People know you care by what you do for them. As opportunities arise I talk about the gospel, salvation and religious questions. My ability in dealing with people helps when it comes to sharing the gospel." Everhart recalls an old adage that says, in effect, what you do speaks louder than what you say.

Helping people began for Everhart when he was brought into the music group doing the nursing home sing-a-long. He saw people with a need and felt something should be done to help them. He also went with a group to help a poor family repair building code violations, finally working alone, hoping to prove he could make a difference in their lives. "I spent five years with this family," says Everhart. "I'm not sure how it finally turned out, but I hope they learned something from me."

"I wanted to be like Jesus," declared Everhart. "I felt I could turn that family around. God doesn't say I need to be successful, but I need to be faithful. I can't let disappointments or apparent failures stop me from doing what I think ought to be done."

There have been times when Everhart says he did not feel like going to a nursing home to visit or sing. Yet, he found that when he went he always felt better afterward, and was glad he went.

Everhart has always been involved in congregational life. He tells how, long ago, he made a pledge to a church building program. He thought it was a good pledge, but soon discovered that his family was not going without something. He decided it wasn't really that great a sacrifice, and since then he has been giving fourteen to eighteen percent of his income to charity.

Besides ministering to others with his gifts, Everhart involves himself in Bible studies and fellowship groups. He finds satisfaction in sharing the joys and sorrows of people in the group.

"I'm still doing the same things I've been doing." says Everhart. "I'm walking down the same old roads." He walks with a sense of calling to service and a satisfaction in his serving.

Dorajean Havrilla
Bookstore Owner

Dorajean Havrilla names service as her calling. "At different times in my life it has been a different service," says Havrilla. "The Lord has called me to serve in different areas throughout my life."

At one time Havrilla started an action group to fight an expansion proposal by a hazardous waste company in the area. She also led a fight against a land fill that was polluting the air with methane gas. She viewed these activities as a service to the community and its people.

Havrilla saw politics as another way to serve, to help people. She felt the Lord called her into politics. She had expressed an interest in politics years before she became involved in a political office. "I prayed for the Lord's guidance about getting into politics," said Havrilla. "The Lord has always answered me through other people." She tells how a neighbor vacated his council seat to run for mayor, and asked her to fill his seat.

Today Havrilla serves the spiritual needs of people through the Christian bookstores she owns and operates. "The stores were started with a focus on ministering to the needs of people," says Havrilla. "They come in with problems, with pain in their lives, and I listen and often pray with them."

The day at each store begins with prayer. The staff prays together for everyone who comes to the store. Customers with specific needs can request prayer in a log book. Meetings with partners, accountants and attorneys begin and end with prayer.

Havrilla says she had a desire for a Christian store for ten years. "When the time was right the Lord called me, with a partner, to start the store in Twinsburg, and a short time later with my husband, Ron, to start the Youngstown store," said Havrilla.

"The Lord showed us the store name and other details. It took six months to get the phone number we wanted for the second store, with JMJ (Jesus, Mary and Joseph) in it. Getting that number is a sign for me that we are supposed to be there."

Havrilla was further affirmed in the decision to open a store in Youngstown when she heard that an ecumenical group there had been praying for a Christian store that would serve the ecumenical community. Both stores were filled with people from the day they opened. Her goal is to bring all Christians together through the stores, helping them minister to others.

Strength for developing this ministry comes from faith, and Havrilla tells about the strengthening of her faith. "Attending a Marriage Encounter weekend with my husband, I discovered a God of love instead of the God of fear I grew up with,"declared Havrilla. "I focused on the Lord. It was a turning point in my life."

Among her gifts, Havrilla names the gift of serving. For her this means a love of people, the ability to deal with people and to resolve problems. She also identifies a strong gift of faith. "I follow what the Lord seems to be showing me," says Havrilla. "Sometimes I don't know the reason why. Sometimes I see it later." A gift of trust goes along with her faith gift. She has put everything, including her house, on the line for the stores.

"I have a lot of discernment that has come through the charismatic gifts,"states Havrilla. "I have been active in a prayer group." She also speaks of a special gift of light. "I get a radiant light when I pray, It's an intense light, it makes pretty colors, and it doesn't matter where I am."

With a strong faith, sensitivity to God's calling and guiding, and a deep prayer life, Havrilla is considering opening a third store. Pursuit of her calling means looking at this possibility to expand her service.

Doug Kirsop
Corporate Quality Manager

Doug Kirsop describes his calling most specifically as helping others to do or to understand something. "I can do many work tasks," says Kirsop. "I can make a big impact, but my call is not to do something directly, but to help others to be able to do it."

Call encompasses all of life for Kirsop, whether it's involvement with church, with other groups he's part of, or at work. It fits everything into one integrated whole.

"Sometimes there's a specific call to do a specific thing for a specific time," states Kirsop. "But my understanding and experience is that call is bigger than that. Understanding and living out our calling as Christians is our primary vocation."

"My understanding and recognition of call is to live it in as many ways as possible," says Kirsop. "The criteria for understanding and recognizing your call is that you enjoy it and don't get burned out. If it's a fit, you can do much more than if you try to do something that is not your calling."

"Call speaks to me in many ways and on many levels — spiritual, intellectual, and emotional," declares Kirsop. "If you're not wired to respond in those ways, I would reassess the call. Calling relates to all parts of life and self."

The Presbyterian church describes itself as reformed and reforming, which means always learning and growing to Kirsop. He finds the question in the Presbyterian ordination service especially meaningful: "Will you serve God's people with energy, imagination, intelligence, and love?" Kirsop says, "You're a student, always learning."

Kirsop's gifts include teaching, training, organizing, and the ability to develop a process to implement those gifts. He also names his ability to see the big picture as a gift, how people and pieces fit together in situations and organizations.

Another gift — relating to people — emerged gradually. Kirsop began his career in the technical field of engineering. "My interest continues and I still develop my engineering skills," says Kirsop. "Now, however, I find a balance between technical things and people. That makes me comfortable with many kinds of people in many situations. I can better understand and communicate with people."

"I envision my gifts as a fulcrum, to use an engineering concept," states Kirsop. "God is the foundation, and the more fully I recognize my gifts the more I become a longer lever. That means the ability to move a lot more weight, in other words to get a lot more done."

Kirsop describes the discernment of his gifts in two phases. In his mid to late teens he began to realize he was both comfortable and effective in organizing and leading groups. The maturity of this gift led to the realization in his thirties that he had the gifts of teaching, training, and organizing.

"Gifts are given for a reason," says Kirsop. "For the most part gifts are not polished when we discover them, but through study and prayer they are further developed and we see more uses for them."

Kirsop likes the concept of sequential calling described by M. Scott Peck in his book *A World Waiting to be Born: Rediscovering Creativity*. A specific calling may be for a time, during which you are prepared for the next calling. Gifts remain constant, but what you've learned leads you to apply them in new situations.

The discernment of calling and gifts is "an ongoing process," says Kirsop. "And we need to be creative participants in that process."

A couple of sayings stick in Kirsop's mind. He remembers hearing people say that God uses those who are closest to God. And from a sermon some years ago by the senior pastor at Bay Presbyterian Church, Bay Village, Ohio: "Sometimes God changes things, but more often God changes people who change things."

Paul Manganiello, M.D.
Medical Doctor

Dr. Paul Manganiello expresses his calling to help people primarily through his medical practice. He has a feeling he could do more than what he does and he struggles with the question of how much he should be doing. "I know I can't do it all," says Manganiello, "but I need to make sure I'm doing enough. There is so much need. Yet, I fear getting in over my head."

"I've always wanted to be a doctor," said Manganiello. "I can't remember a time I did not want to be a physician. In high school all my courses focused on going to college and medical school."

Manganiello recalls how he went through a time when he dropped away from the church. He became disillusioned with what he saw during his years in a parochial school system — the difference between what people said they believed and the way they lived. During his senior year in medical school he started attending church again with his wife to be.

While applying for a medical specialty program, Manganiello remembers staying in a motel room and watching the movie "Jesus of Nazareth." This, he says, got him back in touch with his religious roots. He decided that he needed to be responsible for himself, and not to base his religious life on his reactions to the behavior of others.

Manganiello looks back on this time as going through a phase. It took a while to work it through, taking ownership of his own faith. He became more active in the church from that time.

"I always wanted to have a personal calling," said Manganiello, "a voice, a phone call, a definite clear message." He spent a summer working at a church camp in Mississippi, hoping to hear that clear call. It never came. He was frustrated. As his career in medicine progressed, Manganiello never did experience that "phone call," as he likes to put it. His sense of call emerged as he went along.

Manganiello became active in Bread for the World, an ecumenical advocacy group for the world's hungry. He joined a congregation and soon found himself serving on the church council.

The challenging congregation has helped Manganiello to grow. He has given up listening for "the phone call." The work he does he has come to see as his calling, though he did not plan things this way.

Manganiello says his gift is to help people through medicine. He feels a responsibility to help others, which drew him to medicine. His giftedness as a medical doctor enables him to alleviate suffering.

Another gift Manganiello names is teaching. He passes on his medical knowledge to students and residents. He sees himself as a role model and mentor to young physicians.

A council member, a pious woman, talked about homelessness and challenged the congregation to do something to help. Letters inviting response were sent to other churches. Social service agencies were asked to provide information. A committee was organized which resulted in the formation of an interfaith coalition to provide emergency shelter.

Manganiello then asked about medical care for the homeless, saw the need, and became involved in this ministry. "It just happened," says Manganiello. "I was in the right place at the right time. I just did it. No one told me. I was open and receptive. The call came; it was not planned. I never thought I would be living in northern New England, that was not my intent. Now I see it as directed by God."

Kathleen Manhatten
Artist

Kathleen Manhatten, soft spoken, reflecting a strong commitment in her voice, says God's calling for her life "is to be a sign of God in this world, a window through which people can see God. I feel my presence in the world is to let people see God, but I don't preach and I don't talk much about God. I believe deeply that God shows himself through me."

Following high school graduation, Manhatten became a Catholic sister, a temporary vocation that lasted eleven years. She felt this calling would allow her to let people know about God, but found that she needed a fuller expression of her being and left this vocation. She could have been comfortable in her church role, but needed to leave it in order to become more the person God created her to be.

Art has been a constant in Manhatten's life since she was a small child. She says that art is "a way to express the deeper meaning of everyday things and everyday occurrences. This is how God comes through me." She sees art as a spiritual urging, not to express herself, but to express the deeper meaning of every day.

"Art is basic and spirituality is basic, whether we know it or not, in every person," says Manhatten. "True art carries spirituality on one level or another. It hits the essence of a person. Art comes from our essence and goes to the essence of the other person, it's a spiritual thing."

"I always did art," says Manhatten. "As a child, people enjoyed what I did, smiling, reacting positively, always giving me good comments. I preferred doing art to anything else, discerning early on that art was part of me." She did not think it was anything special, however, thinking anybody could do it. As a result she had no special confidence in her abilities. It came as a surprise to her that other kids could not do art.

In school, teachers asked Manhatten to do different kinds of art, contributing to the discernment of her art talent as a gift. Teachers encouraged her. The high school art teacher was extremely encouraging.

Over a period of years Manhatten came to a point of "deep, deep belief where art, which is a spiritual thing, is part of my connection with God." Between raising children and financial stress in her life, Manhatten often felt guilty about spending time on her art. Through her struggle she came to see that it was more than just using a talent. She felt God was working and expressing himself through her. Her faith deepened. Her bond with God strengthened.

Because of financial stress it was important for Manhatten to sense God's call to do the art, feeling she had to do the art, feeling closed up if she tried not to do it. She describes a longing inside of her for the beauty that underlies life, that there is more to life than what can be seen. People should see God through the art, through the beauty. As she struggled with the tension between the reality of financial stress and doing her art, she came to realize that she had to be true to herself. Her intuition told her to keep at the art.

Another important insight came when Manhatten realized she did not have to do things the way other artists did, but that she had the freedom to find her own artistic expression and value her work on its own merits. She believes that no one work is an artist's "opus mundi" (greatest work), but that every work is an "opus mundi." She continues to grow as an artist, taking the next step such as using a new design, and doing it with excellence. She wants her artistic foundation to be strong. Occasionally she writes a poem to go with a piece she sculpts.

When Manhatten was in college there was a very charismatic teacher she admired and wanted to be like. One day while walking, she thought about what made this teacher so special. A voice from within her told her "it's not what you do or say that matters so much but it's who you are that makes a difference. Art is doing, but the doing has more meaning the more I become who God wants me to be." She sees herself like a small circle in the center of a larger circle which is God.

"When I do what I consider my clearer, from the core, pieces," says Manhatten, "they usually come as a thought or a theme that nags at me. I do a lot of reading or visual stimulation around that theme. Then I go into a period of incubation and let it sit inside of me. All of a sudden it comes out and I do it. It's like God calling me, the partnership between me and God."

Loretta McCartney
Hospital and Hospice Volunteer

Growing up with a physically and verbally abusive, alcoholic father made childhood a nightmare for Loretta McCartney. She lived in constant fear. The two positive influences in her life were wonderful grandparents who were unaware of the stresses she faced, and the church she attended.

McCartney often walked the streets to avoid the threatening atmosphere of home. Life came to a crisis point at age 13. She felt she did not want to live. Walking the streets one evening, deeply depressed, she came upon the church parsonage. Her pastor invited her in and talked with her Then he prayed with her. During that prayer she was filled with an overwhelming feeling of love, a feeling beyond description. The fullness of God's love has been within her ever since. Her home situation did not change, but the love that now filled her, gave her a new way to view life.

McCartney married at 19. She kept her feelings buried and her emotions on the level. She functioned as a secretary and phone receptionist for her husband's home based appliance repair business. She was tied to the house because of the business which kept her husband on the road.

When her husband of 38 years died suddenly, it took McCartney four months to discover what she wanted to do with her life. With absolute certainty she knew what God wanted her to do, to be a caring, compassionate presence to those who hurt.

Warm, caring, sensitive to people's feelings, McCartney began to answer her calling in life by volunteering at the local hospital. She works in the emergency room, sometimes sitting with patients waiting for treatment, sometimes sitting with families waiting for word on loved ones. She offers them comfort.

She has a strong sense of compassion for those who hurt emotionally as well as physically because she experienced so much hurt in her own life.

McCartney volunteered for hospice work in addition to her work at the hospital, going to visit patients while their primary care givers take a break. She usually spends several hours at a time talking with the patients and comforting them. "Some of them have been through a lot," says McCartney. "I have compassion for the patients. I am compelled to do this. I have a strong sense of calling."

McCartney identifies her gifts as compassion and caring. She also has a gift for sensing people's feelings. People affirm McCartney's gifts as they open up to her, knowing her caring and sincerity, especially when they are very ill. She never judges anyone, regardless of what they have done. "Often, dying people need to get things off their chest," says McCartney. "They will not tell their spouse because they do not want to burden them." McCartney is willing to work with aids patients, and she does. Many volunteers will not do that.

McCartney finds that growth comes through her experiences. Learning happens all the time. "It's hard doing this kind of work," says McCartney. "But, I am compelled to do it. It's my calling."

Jean Myers
Bookstore Owner

"My calling uses who I am — my personality, values, traits, wit and a sense of humor," says Jean Myers, owner of Logos Bookstore, a Christian bookstore near Kent State University. "I have a real sensitivity to the Lord working in all areas of my life. My calling goes beyond the bookstore. It's who I am."

The bookstore gives Myers a place to serve. She experiences joy in serving, it keeps her going, energizing what she does. As she seeks to please customers, she feels she receives back what she gives. "Put people first," declares Myers. "You have to do the other things, but people have to be first. We're here to serve one another. We should always have God's love flowing into us and flowing out of us as we share it with others."

Myers sees people from all denominations, giving her a broader view of the church than just one congregation. "I've been so blessed being able to see this broader spectrum."

Logos was founded by several area families with the intention of ministering to students. Myers worked at the store, but also thought about opening a Christian kiosk in a shopping mall. This idea never materialized and she did odd jobs elsewhere. In the meantime, Logos went bankrupt.

Myers and a friend, Becky, went to the board of directors offering to work at the store for no pay for two years. As it worked out, "the Lord gave us the store," said Myers. "Then came the awakening that this is a business."

Myers now works the store alone. "When I'm tired and someone comes in and says how thankful they are that I'm here, it makes a huge difference," states Myers. "I see people with needs come into the store and the right person will always be there. I've seen it happen time and again."

Among her gifts, Myers identifies listening, compassion, and a sense of humor. At age sixteen she taught Sunday School and was involved with children's clubs and a youth group. "I recognized I had a gift of compassion. I was very concerned about people."

Myers considers listening an important gift. "People don't take time to listen," says Myers. "We need to be still, and reflect on life. The trials and the hard times as well as the joyful times are all part of what God has put into us." A sense of humor means Myers doesn't sweat the small stuff.

Affirmations of her calling and gifts come in various ways. A friend pops into the store once in a while and affirms Myers' sense of judgment, her ability to see situations clearly.

When her children were growing up, "their friends used to call, not to talk to them," says Myers, "but to talk to me. I think they needed someone to listen. That was affirming. My gift of listening continues to be affirmed in the store." Myers also finds God affirming her giftedness in little ways.

In her twenties, Myers had thyroid problems, but didn't know what it was. With children at home, she wondered what lay ahead. "Then the Lord gave me a Psalm verse," said Myers. "In your old age you will bear fruit." That became her window to the future.

Myers says that what is needed today is "to focus on Christ, to forget what's behind and press on to the calling, to stand in awe of the God who has chosen us."

Timothy Nealon
Manager

When Timothy Nealon began his career with Higbee's, now Dillard's, Department Store, he envisioned himself climbing the career ladder, receiving regular promotions, transferring often to new locations, finally reaching the executive suite. He watched as this pattern developed in the lives of managers who worked for him; but for his own life this pattern did not develop.

Now, as manager of Dillard's regional distribution center in Cleveland, Nealon sees his calling "to help other people to develop in their business careers and in their lives." This is not what he had in mind for himself, but what he believes God had in mind for him. Reflecting on his life, "this is what God had me do," said Nealon. "God entrusted me with these lives, to serve as a mentor to them."

"I feel called to take what I hear preached in the pulpit and attempt to apply those principals in my daily life," says Nealon. "I take with me what was said and live it."

"As for gifts," declares Nealon, "I have been blessed with common sense." Common sense told Nealon that teaching Sunday School was not for him. Instead, he took his administrative ability and began using his business skills in the church. Administration is where he feels he fits best.

"My role in organizations is to cause those organizations to focus on what their mission is, or to identify their mission if they haven't done so," says Nealon. "I want to be able to shape the direction of the organization I'm part of."

Nealon respects other people's beliefs, even if he does not agree. He gives his employees a lot of freedom in making decisions. That is what helped them develop," said Nealon. "I saw what was good in them and had them exploit that."

"My gift of common sense meant telling some people that I didn't think retailing was their thing," said Nealon. On one occasion he told an employee that retailing was not right for him. The man called him the next day and said, "you're right. I'm changing careers." Today that man is a fine, successful attorney, and is doing very well.

This event made Nealon aware of the need to be certain about what he tells people. "People listen," says Nealon. "I am very careful about what I tell people, because I want to be sure I am as accurate as possible in what I say."

"God answers prayer," states Nealon. "When he does, it's such a neat feeling — that God is present and available."

Jim Petersen
Executive Director for Ministries

"I have a passion for reaching people with the gospel," says Jim Petersen. "I believe God has called me to put my gifts of visioning, futuristics, being able to see the big picture in a different way, research, interviewing, presenting, speaking, preaching, graphics, and video production, to work in some rather unique ways that benefit the church."

Currently Petersen serves as Executive Director for Ministries at Community Lutheran Church in Las Vegas, Nevada, heading the evangelism team, teaching, and preaching. Previously, he served with the Division for Congregational Ministries of the Evangelical Lutheran Church in America. He worked with the Education-Evangelism Team's interactive workshops; "Awakening, Disciple!, Renewed!, Restored!," and "Choices," that allow someone to introduce a congregation to ideas that are working in other congregations through video and discussion techniques. "I dreamed up the technique and have done the travel, research and production," said Petersen. As an Associate Director for Evangelism with the ELCA, on the Education-Evangelism Team, "I had specific responsibility for spreading the eleven Church Membership Initiative studies on why Lutheran congregations grow or don't grow throughout the denomination. It was a wonderful time of both learning and disseminating information."

"My calling and my gifts were discerned at different times," stated Petersen. "My calling was discerned first. I was reared in a Christian home, but during college wandered away. Though my wife brought me back to church and I became active, I was still pretty much a Sunday morning 'pew potato.'" A series of health related events, covering a five year period, ended with the death of his parents. His wife was bedridden for almost a year when their children were in junior and senior high school, "bringing me to the realization that even in the deepest valleys of that time in life, the one rock solid thing that remained in my life was my faith."

Petersen came out of those experiences determined to change the way he lived and to commit his life to Christ. "I made a list of my gifts, and began to try to figure out how to put them to work for the Lord," stressed Petersen. "About that time my pastor said to me one Sunday morning, 'you know Jim, since you've been serving on the committee for a new Lutheran Church, you really ought to look at some ways you could put your gifts to work in the new ELCA.'" Petersen obtained a list of possible positions, applied, was hired, and began to work for the ELCA in August, 1988.

"I think that many times we don't know whose lives we touch and influence," says Petersen. "That's the wonderful thing about what I do. Even now, as an ELCA Evangelism Partner, I travel all over the country doing workshops, seminars and video taping, and meet literally hundreds of Lutherans. And I hear back from many of them. But I'd feel fulfilled even if I didn't hear from anyone because I know that what I do now counts for something."

"For a while I felt like God had taken a 2 x 4 to get my attention," he said. "Today, I keep looking and listening for 'clues' that will give me another entre to share the gospel story with people, pastors and congregations."

Among people who were influential for Petersen, was Dr. Edward Lindemann, president emeritus of Whitworth College in Spokane, Washington, and a Christian futurist. Meeting at an American Lutheran Church district convention in Kansas City in 1977, "Dr. Lindemann actually began the process that changed my life," said Petersen. "I was so fascinated by his presentation, I called him, arranged to follow him around campus for two days, bought a plane ticket to Spokane and went. He became my first mentor and began the process of making me think about my life — interestingly — just two years before that difficult five year stretch hit."

Among other influential people were Petersen's parents who began the day in their home with Bible study and prayer at breakfast, a local pastor at a church camp when he was 15, his wife who brought him back to church, and his pastor who suggested he apply for the ELCA position.

"The Christian walk is a journey and not a destination," declares Petersen. "So I'm on this exciting and compelling path that is always full of surprises."

Pam Pollack
Wife and Mother

Pam Pollack says that her childhood dream for her future was to stay at home, have children, and care for them. She values children as most important to God. She raises her children to love God. "My priority is to be with my children," says Pollack, "to be there for their needs and to teach them."

"When my first child was born I felt it was a validation that God exists," declares Pollack. "There is nothing greater than seeing the newborn and how miraculous they are. It was shortly afterward that I became more intent in pursuing God, wanting to know God better."

Getting involved in learning and spiritual growth opportunities in her church led Pollack to attend a parish renewal weekend in 1992. "This was an eye opening event, a turning point, a conversion experience," said Pollack. "I always felt close to God, but this experience opened my eyes." Her husband, Joe, had a similar experience. He lightened his load at work so he could spend more time at home and help raise their children. A son in sixth grade is being home schooled.

"Bearing children, sharing in the fullness of life and bringing a child into being is a unique way to serve God," says Pollack. "Children remind me that I need to be like a child before the Lord."

"The biggest decision I faced was whether to continue to have more children," states Pollack. "My husband wanted to stop at three because of our ages and because of his job related travel. We decided we would accept whatever the Lord might show us. Only the Lord can give life." Another child is on the way.

Her calling to motherhood led Pollack to become involved in the Right to Life movement. She tearfully shares the story of a woman she knew who died recently. The woman, a diabetic, was pregnant with her second child. Doctors said she wouldn't live and should terminate the pregnancy. She persisted in having the child, now a healthy twenty-three year old. She was hospitalized three weeks following the delivery as doctors fought to keep her out of a diabetic coma. Her commitment to having that child reinforced Pollack's own sense of call and determination to become more active in pro life work as her own children grow more independent.

Among her gifts, Pollack highlights a love for children, having a heart for people, and a great love for God. "This gives me more love for my family, strength, and more patience to understand the children," says Pollack. "God is very abundant when I ask. When I forget to ask, things don't go so well."

Pollack spends time studying the teachings of the church. She finds they encourage her gift of motherhood, feeling she is cooperating with God in giving and guiding life.

Personal and family prayer are also important for Pollack. She relies heavily on prayer. "I try to listen to the little voice I hear when I pray. I try to be like Christ. I find strength in the Virgin Mary."

Pollack has been involved in a church program that focuses on the work of God, teaching the value of everyday tasks. "There are talks on the value of everyday life even though some things seem mundane and repetitious," reports Pollack. "It makes me feel like I am important. I serve God in what I do."

Influential people in Pollack's life include her husband, Joe, a support group at church, Godly friends, and other mothers who understand the value of being at home. Her social life revolves around her church. "The Lord has blessed us," says Pollack. " We tithe at church, and try to do more."

Mary Ann Sima
Volunteer in Youth Ministry

Anywhere youth ministry happens in the Northeastern Ohio Synod of the Evangelical Lutheran Church in America, Mary Ann Sima can be found, always with a smile and a warm enthusiastic greeting. With her husband Jim, a great deal of time, energy and self goes into youth work.

Various experiences form Sima's calling in youth ministry. From the time she was young there was a sense of calling to do the Lord's work. She thought about becoming a pastor, but when she graduated from high school in 1968 women pastors were not permitted in the Lutheran church.

At that time, women who wanted to work in the church could be musicians, or be pastor's wives heavily involved in their husband's congregations. Neither musically inclined nor a pastor's wife, opportunities to serve the Lord seemed very limited.

While in high school Sima attended a church sponsored Leadership Training School. One activity sent participants into an urban neighborhood by themselves to knock on doors and ask residents about their faith and how they viewed the changing community. She felt, "I can't do that," but she did. Even though frightening, she says it was a growth experience.

A summer vacation during college took her to Luther Memorial Camp in central Ohio. Part of the summer was spent helping staff a Vacation Bible School at a church in a changing neighborhood in Columbus. Visits to a Salvation Army center and other social ministry sites provided greater awareness of urban life. She shared her experiences with the adult Sunday School class at her church on return, building confidence in her public speaking ability.

Some years later, Sima responded to a plea for help with the seventh and eighth grade confirmation classes. "I saw a need," said Sima. "No one else was doing it."

Her congregation entered a difficult time. It was hard to get people to do things. The nominating committee, meeting across the room from where she was serving coffee on a Sunday morning, asked her to run for council and become president of the congregation. She accepted the invitation.

The pastor accepted another call, leaving the congregation just before the constituting assembly of the Northeastern Ohio Synod. As president, she led the congregational discussions about the new church body, adding to her leadership experience.

During the pastoral vacancy Sima worked with the interim pastor who was a seminary graduate not yet ordained. She showed him ministry needs in the congregation. In the process she learned a lot about the synod and the workings of the church. "You grow when you help someone else," says Sima.

During this time her work in youth ministry grew. Formation of a high school Sunday School class led to involvement in youth activities. In local and national youth events she gave more time and energy. She sees youth work as an important way to support her daughters, who are involved in local and national leadership, in youth events in the Evangelical Lutheran Church in America. She says her church always has one of the largest groups of any church at regional youth events.

Sima considers her greatest gift "empathy for kids." Many young people from the community consider themselves part of the youth group. Each year several of them join the church.

"You can never become complacent," states Sima. "The group changes as youth graduate and go to college. New, younger people come into the group."

Sima often receives letters from the college students saying how important their faith is and how much their time in the youth group meant to them. "I find youth work exciting," she added. "You can always see God working in their lives."

"Being willing to share what God does in your life and accepting kids for who they are," says Sima, "is the key to youth ministry. There is no special training or education for that."

Youth ministry differs greatly from Sima's idea in college that she would like to teach math or science in high school or college. Is she disappointed at how things turned out? Not at all. She still gets to teach high school and confirmation classes. Only the subject matter is different.

"We like to have a set path," declares Sima, "but we need to be open to what God wants us to be and do."

Sir John M. Templeton
John Templeton Foundation

Sir John Templeton stands as a giant in the investment world. Hailed as the most successful investor of all time during his guest appearances on television's popular financial program Wall Street Week, he uses these opportunities to promote spirituality as well as principles for sound investing. His optimistic outlook on life and enthusiasm for what he does show strongly in his writing and speaking. But there's a special spark when he talks about spirituality.

Founder and manager of the Templeton mutual fund family, he sold his firm, near his 80th birthday, for a reported $500,000,000. Freed from business responsibilities, Templeton could devote full time and energy to promote his long held interest in religion and spirituality. To this end he founded the John Templeton Foundation in 1987 "to explore and encourage the link between the sciences and all religions."

The John Templeton Foundation Fact Sheet states, "the best known of the Foundation's programs, The Templeton Prize for Progress in Religion, was established in 1972 to address the absence of a Nobel prize for achievement in religion." The prize, awarded annually, is worth $1,000,000. Among the better known winners are the late Mother Theresa and the Rev. Billy Graham.

The following quotations from The Templeton Prize booklet highlight the intentions of the prize. "This award is intended to encourage the concept that resources and manpower are needed for progress in spiritual knowledge. We hope that by learning about the lives of the awardees, millions of people will be uplifted and inspired to be enthusiastic about the further study and worship of God."

"It is hoped that there will result from this enterprise a deeper spiritual awareness on the part of humankind, a better understanding of the meaning of life, heightened quality of devotion and love, and a greater emphasis on the kind of dedication that brings the human life more into concert with the divine will, thus releasing new and creative energies into human society today."

The Foundation funds more than 40 areas of endeavor. They fall into three broad categories: science and religion; spirituality and health; and education. Templeton dreams that the world would one day devote at least one tenth of the estimated two billion dollars a day it spends on research in science and medicine to research on spiritual subject matter.

Templeton says, "God's calling for my life may be to find ways to use for God's purposes the talents God gives each of us. Everyone has a wide variety of God given talents which can be discovered by diligent search." For Templeton, these include simple common sense, a strong work ethic and the ability to do two tasks simultaneously. For 65 years he worked more than 60 hours a week.

More specifically, "God may have given me talents to use common sense in selecting profitable investments for people and for charities such as Princeton Theological Seminary," says Templeton. Proof of his giftedness can be seen in the solid performance of the Templeton funds. For instance, a $10,000 investment in the Templeton Growth Fund at its inception in 1954 would have grown to $2,289,272 by March 31, 1995.

Templeton brought similar results to the endowment fund of Princeton Theological Seminary as a trustee and later as chairman of the Board of Trustees. When he retired from the Board several years ago he taught the members how to invest, said the Rev. Chase S. Hunt, Director of Planned Giving for Princeton Seminary. The outstanding results have continued.

Of his personal giving, Templeton disclosed, "for half a century my donations to religions and charities were at least ten percent. Now through the blessings of God, my program is to donate, each year, 50 times as much as I spend on myself."

Prayer and reading helped Templeton the most in discovering his talent. The key event that influenced the development of his gifts and calling was "that day as a sophomore at Yale when my father told me the Great Depression made him unable to give me even one dollar more," said Templeton. "This seeming tragedy was a divine blessing because it taught me self reliance, ingenuity and the ability to do more than one task at the same time."

Templeton's concerns in religion and spirituality spill over into a genuine concern for the improvement of the human condition. "Most people get joy from alleviating the suffering of others but it is even more useful to research and reduce the causes of suffering," says Templeton. "Such research and business competition have resulted in over 100 fold increase in output per person of goods and services in less than two centuries. Such wonderful acceleration is even more rapid in the field of information than in material goods and services."

Further insights into Templeton's philosophy can be gained from his book, *The Templeton Plan: 21 Steps to Personal Success and Real Happiness*. The focus on giving, growing, spirituality and the betterment of others underlie the principles outlined.

"Finally," states Templeton, "common sense should tell everyone that usefulness and happiness and also personal prosperity come not from selfishness, but more usually from trying diligently to serve others, especially through higher quality and lower cost services and products."

Christopher Turgeon
High School Student

Christopher Turgeon considers God's calling in his life to be "to help others in times of need and for just cause, to give my assistance to others when I can help, and to be happy and cheerful and to look for the positive in everything."

Turgeon tries to carry out God's calling in his life in everything he does. Some experiences include helping his classmates with math or any other subject he can offer assistance on, helping his high school's student council clean a section of highway, and helping an elderly couple with yard work and other needs. "I like to help others in need," says Turgeon. "It makes me feel good to know that I helped them accomplish something they couldn't do on their own."

Among the many gifts God has given him, Turgeon says his health is the greatest gift. Other gifts include his drive and motivation, his friendliness and happiness, his willingness to help others, his search for joy in everything he does, and his ability to counsel others and listen to their problems which he considers very important. His help extends to classmates, neighbors and people in the community.

"I discerned my calling and gifts when I talked to others about myself," said Turgeon. "What I mean is that it took me to look at myself from someone else's perspective to see what was special about myself. I kind of had a clue to begin with, but their point of view verified it for me."

Turgeon tells how he gained a key insight. "One day I was helping my mom out when she worked in a nursing home and I saw an elderly man having problems with some bags. I offered my assistance but he didn't take it. I pondered this reaction for a while and concluded that he just wanted to do it himself and didn't want others to think he was too old. This made it clear that some people don't want help."

Turgeon tells about how he gained another insight into himself. "An event that made my positive outlook clear to me was when I fell asleep behind the wheel. I was on the interstate and had fallen asleep. I drifted from one side of the highway to the other. Thank God there were no other cars on the highway at that time. When I hit the guard rails I woke up and stopped. I thought about what had just happened and realized how lucky I was to have hit the guardrails and not gone into the gutter between the lanes of the highway. Other adolescents might have been mad that they dented and scraped their car."

"My mom has played a major role in my discerning my gifts, and she was the one who taught me right from wrong," said Turgeon. "Pastor John Crilley, Community Lutheran Church, Enfield, New Hampshire, also played a big role. He always has something happy and inspiring to say to you, always making you feel better. I've taken Pastor Crilley's cheerfulness and applied it to my life. So far, it has proven to be helpful in the way I not only deal with events in my life but help others with theirs. I don't like to be sad or mad so I think of something happy or positive and it helps me get along."

But life has not always been easy. "There have been times when I've had to choose between right and wrong when asked to do something with my friends," declared Turgeon. "I've chosen the right path just about all the time. It's really hard to go against your friends in these types of situations."

Turgeon has found affirmation of his calling and gifts coming from his parents, friends, and people in the community. "People's reactions mean a lot to me," says Turgeon. "I like to help others and often do it without even knowing. I do not find it hard and enjoy doing it, so I guess that's a big clue for me."

In addition to school, Turgeon works in a store, a good place to live out his calling to help others. "This allows me to talk to a lot of people. We joke around and sometimes talk serious about things. People have been great to me, and I thank them for it."

Reed Walters
Computer Analyst, Church Musician

Reed Walter's day job as a computer systems analyst provides income so he can pursue his calling as a church musician. He leads people in contemporary worship experiences with the praise group he directs, Hearts Afire. As worship leader he gets people involved. The group uses mostly songs that people can easily join in singing.

"Worship is not a spectator sport," says Walters. "We're going to sing at a prison, and we will invite the prisoners to sing along, not just sing to them."

Hearts Afire wants to express the joy of being God's people through its music. Through the sing-a-long songs, people are invited to experience that joy.

Walters' calling became clear gradually over the years. "Opportunities presented themselves," said Walters. "Doors seemed to open at the right time, I was qualified, and it seemed a good way to serve the Lord. I enjoy what I'm doing now. Yet, if God has a change in mind I'm sure it would be something I would enjoy more."

Calling for Walters did not mean pursuing opportunities; the opportunities pursued him. There was no grand plan, but a continued sensitivity to the Lord's leading and calling, coming to see the potential of opportunities that opened before him.

Walters traces his sense of calling. "I was brought up Lutheran, drifted away, and in college was brought back to the Lord by Charismatic Catholics," said Walters. "I got involved in the Lay Witness Mission of a United Methodist Church, going with teams to other congregations, because I played the guitar and the keyboard. The leaders were Methodist but the team members were from many denominations. I began to feel a calling to this."

Most ministry work Walters has done focused more on those already churched rather than on the unchurched. He finds the idea of being a roving musician appealing. "How do I know where God wants me to go next?" asks Walters with a glint in his eye and a smile on his face. "I go through open doors. It beats going through closed doors. I feel blessed. I get to meet so many different people."

At various times Walters served as a church organist, spending eighteen years in that capacity at Lord of Life Lutheran Church, Chagrin Falls, Ohio. "It was a tough decision to leave Lord of Life, but I felt like it was time to move on, even though I didn't know where," said Walters. "I had no plans to join the praise group at that time. I once said I would never lead people in singing like that, but God changed my mind. Change seems to be one constant in life."

Among his gifts, Walters names music, the ability to play various instruments, composing, a decent singing voice, and parents with the resources and willingness to get him the lessons he needed to develop his musical abilities. He feels he was also given safe settings in which to put his gifts to use, starting in high school to work as a church organist.

"I never had a problem with stage fright," says Walters. "I could always get up in front of people easily. For the calling I have that's kind of important."

Walters has played for community services at all of the Auburn Bainbridge Council of Churches congregations: Lutheran, Catholic, Presbyterian, and United Church of Christ. "It's neat to experience the breadth of God's family," states Walters. "Hearts Afire performs in churches of all denominations and I feel the love of God for all people."

"I think the only way you retire from God's service is feet first," says Walters. "God has been a good boss."

Wendy Widdersheim
Liturgical Dancer

"My calling as a liturgical dancer became clear in the last two years," declared Wendy Widdersheim. "A friend had talked to me about looking at patterns in my life."

Widdersheim enjoys being in churches and libraries. She feels a sense of peace and security in churches. "I recognized that I function out of a spiritual direction," said Widdersheim. "Yet, I felt odd about it because it seemed so unusual."

"I always feel I honor God best in a serving role," says Widdersheim. "I have a servants heart that keeps growing stronger." Her satisfaction in serving goes back to an experience with a Youth Fellowship group when she was in ninth grade. For a project they went to clean the basement of an inner city church. It was a lot of work but it produced a good feeling.

Widdersheim's first experience with liturgical dance came while she was a college student performing at a nearby church. Her next experience came several years later when, at age 25, she got involved in a church and liturgical dance. Then came a longer break in her dance activities, lasting until she was 39. This time her involvement in a touring liturgical dance group lasted five or six years before tapering off. "It was neat to be in churches," said Widdersheim "The group was always introduced as peacemakers, fitting in with my sense of mission."

Once, at a mission conference, Widdersheim heard the words, "whoever would be great among you must be a servant." This started her on a search for truth. She felt that life could be better, that life doesn't have to remain the way it is.

"I struggled with some difficult times, moving toward God, finding peace, then moving away again," stated Widdersheim. "A turning point came during a battle with depression. I felt I didn't want to dance again. I had the experience of God reaching his hand in and pulling me out. It's like I finally believe, and I know the Bible is the Word of God."

"Where you're called to serve, you will sense a right fit," says Widdersheim. "When I tried to succeed at serving myself I fell flat on my face. When things came to me and I felt called to them, I functioned well. I can't force myself into things. It doesn't work."

Widdersheim was putting her dance things away a year ago when she felt called to dance again. "I feel ready to go on with my mission," exclaims Widdersheim. "I sort through Scripture to seek direction. I feel I am now called to teach movement in music. I am also involved in a musical production, 'Godspell,' finding a lot of my prior learning and experience coming together. I am a child of God. I am an artist. That awareness makes it easier for me to see what God wants me to do." She sees her involvement in the liturgical dance group as a way to share her faith, dancing as liturgy, as a way of presenting the gospel.

Among her gifts, Widdersheim includes: creativity; accepting people for who they are and seeing children for who they can be; resourcefulness; service; the ability to see a need and address it; being a good listener; and putting her whole self into what she does.

"I'm learning discernment now," states Widdersheim. "I need to wait to hear what's to come next. The time of waiting is a time to rest and renew. I anticipate that God will continue to use me."

Gerald W. Bauer
Pastor, Author, Teacher

My calling is to use my public speaking and writing gifts to communicate God's presence to the spiritually hungry. I carry out my calling through teaching, preaching and writing. I also use these gifts in the broader realm where they provide opportunity for witness

When teaching nonprofit organization management seminars I need to use examples. Taking illustrations from my pastoral ministry experience provides a way of witnessing to Christ's presence without getting into separation of church and state problems.

It works in a similar way with writing. When interviewing people for profile articles, it's easy to ask if there are Christian values that inform their lives. I believe the witness of Christians in the work-a-day world is significant. People don't expect it, and when they hear and see it I think it makes a big impact.

God has given me a number of gifts. I see public speaking and writing gifts as primary. They serve as ways of using and giving expression to the other gifts.

Discernment of calling and gifts began during high school. Always active in church, it was at a church camp following my junior year that I first sensed God's calling. At camp there was an emphasis on the ministry. I admired my pastor. I would envision myself leading worship or preaching the sermon, but I never considered the ministry as a career until it was suggested at camp.

After several years in the ministry, I experienced a restlessness that was satisfied only for a short time with calls to other congregations. Prayerful deliberation led to a decision to pursue interests in charitable giving and investments as a different way of doing ministry.

This new career lasted a short two years. The Lord had other plans for me. Looking back, I can see how, if I had been successful in financial services, I would have missed tremendous spiritual, intellectual and personal growth.

Part-time interim pastoral work and a part-time pastorate followed. A good deal of time was spent at Capital University's Cleveland Center teaching religion, history, and the management of nonprofit organizations, and in the Religious Studies department at John Carroll University. Writing became more prominent during this time.

Those years of financial uncertainty were also years of growth. I learned a lot from every one of those different experiences. Most important, I came to see how the Lord was using each one to bring me to a stronger faith and deeper trust in his leading and providing. The Lord's timing and attention to detail in my life are absolutely amazing.

All along I have received affirmation of my speaking and writing gifts. But I have not been sure what role my writing should have. The turning point in writing came as I interviewed people for this book. Their stories were more than just what happened in the discernment of their calling. Their profiles were faith stories, revealing God at work in their lives. I was captivated and motivated by their stories. These stories demanded to be told. The book became a mission and I developed a sense of urgency about the need to get this witness into print and into the hands of readers. Writing the book became for me a way to give, a way to serve, a way to do ministry.

At this time I sense God calling me to three areas of service. I am called to continue doing interim pastoral work, to continue teaching seminars oriented to both the church and nonprofit organizations, and to develop a writing ministry. I know the Lord guides and empowers me as I follow the Lord's invitation to serve.

CONCLUSION

I

Several themes appear in the profiles. These people have a passion for their calling. Whether paid or volunteer, they have a sense of purpose. They radiate warmth, an energy for what they do. They reflect a sense of self confidence. Their voices are lively and upbeat. There is a contagious excitement in being around them.

The people profiled focus on giving of themselves to help others. They use their energy to make life better for those who can benefit from the gifts of their calling. They show a strong conviction that God calls them to give of themselves. They are committed to living their callings in life.

Many of the people profiled experienced some type of crisis. Some crises were brief, some lengthy, some came as a series of events. The crisis often played a role in their discernment of calling, usually apparent in looking back.

Some of the profiles suggest that early involvement in an activity related to an interest was influential in discerning giftedness and calling. This makes it helpful, especially for young people, to have opportunities to pursue an area of interest, to try some things that are available as a way of testing the sense of call.

II

A few concluding thoughts for your discernment journey emerge from the stories. An openness to what the Lord will reveal, and a sense of expectation and anticipation, prepares you to discern opportunities for service and direction of call. Be alert for signs of God's moving in your life.

God comes to you in the context of your own experiences, personality, abilities, and interests. God works in your life in ways that are best suited to who you are, inviting you to become increasingly the person God created you to be.

You can take this journey of self discovery in confidence, knowing you are in God's hands. As you continue your journey to discern your God given calling and gifts, may you emerge and blossom into the fullness of life.

RESOURCES

The resources listed here are those cited in the text. I have used them all and found them to be helpful.

Books

Richard N. Boles, *What Color is Your Parachute*.
   Published by Ten Speed Press, revised annually. The definitive book in the field of job changing, career planning, and life assessment. Includes a directory of resources.

Gary L. Harbaugh, *God's Gifted People: Discovering Your Personality as a Gift*.
   Published by Augsburg in 1990, uses the Myers-Briggs Type Indicator as a basis for applying giftedness to life settings. Accurate results are achieved using the exercises in the book. Examples of how people of different personality types lived their giftedness focuses on congregational settings, but the applications can easily be applied in other areas.

Ronald Klug, *How to Keep a Spiritual Journal*.
   An Augsburg publication, contains a comprehensive overview of spiritual journal writing. Very practical, easy to use. A good introductory book on the subject.

Organization

Intercristo

This Seattle based organization functions in three areas: self study course on career change and job search; career planning seminars; and a global job bank listing positions in Christian organizations.

Intercristo
19303 Freemont Avenue North
P.O. Box 33487
Seattle, WA 98133
Ph.: 1-800-251-7740